Travellers' Guide to the French Menu

GW00691801

Travellers' Guide to the
French
MENU

Absolute Press

Published by
Absolute Press (Publishers)
14 Widcombe Crescent, Bath, Avon. BA2 6AH.

© Absolute Press (Publishers)

First published 1985

Edited and Compiled by **Gill Rowley**

Illustrations Carl Willson

Cover printed by
Kennet & Avon Printing Company Limited,
26 Brock Street, Bath.

Text photoset and printed by
Photobooks (Bristol) Limited,
Barton Manor, St. Philips, Bristol.

Bound by W.H. Ware & Son Limited,
Tweed Road Industrial Estate,
Clevedon, Avon.

ISBN 0 9506785 9 7

Contents

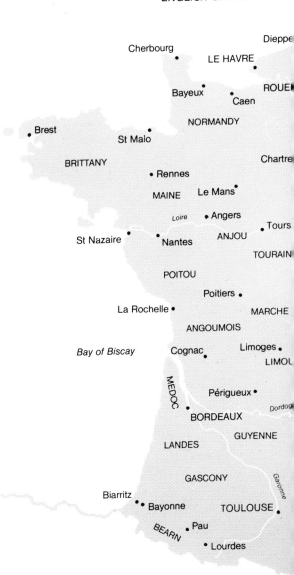

ENGLISH CHANNEL

Cherbourg
Dieppe
LE HAVRE
Bayeux
ROUEN
Caen
NORMANDY

Brest
St Malo
BRITTANY
Chartres
Rennes
MAINE
Le Mans
Loire
Angers
Tours
St Nazaire
Nantes
ANJOU
TOURAINE
POITOU
Poitiers
La Rochelle
MARCHE
ANGOUMOIS
Bay of Biscay
Cognac
Limoges
LIMOU
MEDOC
Périgueux
Dordogne
BORDEAUX
GUYENNE
LANDES
GASCONY
Garonne
Biarritz
Bayonne
TOULOUSE
BEARN
Pau
Lourdes

SPAIN

Introduction

The cuisine of the French is not one cuisine but many. There is the traditional *haute cuisine* of the grand restaurants and hotels, with its rich sauces and lavish use of expensive ingredients such as butter, cream, truffles, wines and spirits. There is French home cooking – perhaps heartier, certainly less rich, but still executed with the utmost care (even at family level, cooking and eating are regarded respectively as an art and a great joy of life). Then there is the upstart newcomer, *la nouvelle cuisine*, which proved that superb dishes can be created without the use of cholesterol-laden ingredients and extolled the virtues of exquisite presentation over quantity. The Japanese have always known this, of course, but the French hailed the discovery as their own and put their own Gallic stamp on it.

Yet this is not all: France is many regions, each with its own individual character and its own specialities. You will eat a very different type of meal in Alsace from the type you would eat on the Provençal coast and that would be quite different again from the food of Bourgogne or of Brittany. You will also find foreign influences – France's associations with North Africa have made *couscous* widely popular and you will find *paella* and *pizza*, to say nothing of the ubiquitous hamburger restaurants, throughout the country.

There is much to explore in this land of 'foodies', and wherever you eat in France you will benefit from the fact that the French are very discerning restaurant customers. You will also see, particularly at lunchtime on Sundays, whole families, often three generations, out enjoying their favourite *biftek* with mountains of *frites* and a steady flow of red wine.

While you are in France, have a wander round the food-stores as well as eating in the restaurants. It will tell you a lot about French food and also help you to find your way around the restaurant menus – for which purpose I hope you will find this little book useful.

Phrases for the Restaurant

I want to reserve a table for . . . . . . at . . . . . .
Je voudrais réserver une table pour . . . . . . à . . . . . .
Have you a table for . . . . . .
Avez-vous une table pour . . . . . .
A quiet table
Une table dans un coin tranquil, s'il vous plaît
A table near the window
Une table près de la fenêtre
A table on the terrace
Une table sur la terrasse
Could we have another table please?
Nous voudrions changer de table, s'il vous plaît?
I am in a hurry/we are in a hurry
Je suis pressé/Nous sommes pressés
Please bring me the menu
Apportez-moi le menu, s'il vous plaît
Can we have a . . . . . . please
Nous voulons un . . . . . . s'il vous plaît
Local dishes
Plats régionaux
How much is it?
Combien ça coûte?
What is it?
Qu'est-ce que c'est que ça?
I did not order this
Ce n'est pas ça que j'ai commandé
Too much
C'est trop
More
Un peu plus
The bill please
L'addition, s'il vous plaît
Is service included?
Est-ce que le service est compris?
I think there is a mistake in the bill
Je pense qu'il y a une erreure dans l'addition
Do you accept travellers' cheques?
Acceptez-vous les chèques de voyage?

Restaurant Terms

addition
bill

apéritif
drink taken before the meal (to stimulate the appetite)

bistro, bistrot
café, small restaurant

brasserie
restaurant serving meals, snacks and drinks, usually from early morning to late at night

carte
menu; *à la*, choice of entire menu

commande, sur
('on request'), cooked to order

compris
included

couvert
cover (charge)

crêperie
restaurant serving mainly *crêpes*

déjeuner
lunch

dessert
dessert

dîner
dinner

entrée
main course

garçon, monsieur
waiter

hors d'oeuvre
appetizer, starter

menu
fixed-price menu, as opposed to *à la carte*

pichet
flask for wine

plat du jour
  dish of the day
prix fixe
  set price (menu)
petit déjeuner
  breakfast
restaurant
  restaurant
service compris
  service included
souper
  supper
table
  table; *d'hôte* (host's table), fixed-price menu of
  several courses
verre
  glass

Menu Terms

abats
offal

abricot
apricot

agneau
lamb; *de lait*, baby; *pascal* (Easter), spring

aigre
sour, bitter

aigre-doux
sweet and sour

aiguillette
sliver, particularly from the breast (poultry or game);
also top part of rump (beef)

aiglefin
haddock

ail
garlic

aile
wing (on poultry)

aileron
tip of the wing (on poultry)

aïllade
pertaining to a dish made with garlic; also a garlic
mayonnaise, with tomatoes and herbs

aïoli, ailloli
type of mayonnaise containing a good deal of garlic
(also, optionally, breadcrumbs); in the Midi, com-
plete dish with cod, snails and vegetables

air, en l'
puffed, puffs

Albert
creamy horseradish sauce

Albertine
sauce for fish made with white wine, mushrooms
and truffles

albigeoise, à l'
in the style of Albi, in the Languedoc, with stuffed

tomatoes, ham and potatoes

Albuféra

see *caneton*

allumettes

'matchsticks', very thin-cut potatoes or pastry puffs

alose

shad, speciality of the Gironde, often grilled; sometimes stuffed with sorrel

alsacienne, à l'

Alsace-style, often indicating the presence of pickled cabbage (*choucroute*) and/or *foie gras*; or potatoes; or sausage; otherwise madeira sauce, truffles, noodles and *foie gras*

amande

almond

amandin(e)

almond-flavoured

américaine

American; see also *armoricaine*

ananas

pineapple

anchois

anchovy

andouilles

black-skinned sausages made from pork tripe, served cold

andouillettes

sausage made from pork intestine, served hot with mustard

anglaise, a l'

in the English style; various meanings, e.g. served plain, or boiled, or (of fish) dipped in beaten eggs and coated in breadcrumbs

anguille

eel; *aux pruneaux*, sautéed, cooked in wine, with prunes (speciality of Brittany and the Pays Nantais); *au vert*, with white wine and green herbs, served cold (speciality of Lille)

ardennaise, à l'

Ardennes-style, with juniper berries

argenteuil

soup (*crème*) or other dish containing asparagus

Armagnac

brandy, from Gascony, similar in style and quality to Cognac

armoricaine, à l'

(sometimes, incorrectly, *américaine*) Breton-style (Armorica is Brittany); sauce, especially for lobster, containing white wine, cognac, tomatoes and butter

artichauts

globe artichokes; *à la bretonne* (Brittany-style),

with cider and onions; *favorite*, with asparagus and cheese; *fonds d'*, bottoms

asperges

asparagus; *à la flamande* (Flanders-style), with a butter and egg-yolk sauce

assiette anglaise

('English plate'), dish of assorted cold meats, perhaps with gherkins to garnish, served as an appetizer

assorti

mixed, assorted

aubergine

aubergine

Aurore

velouté sauce with tomato (named after his mother by Brillat-Savarin)

auvergnate, à l'

Auvergne-style, often denoting the presence of cabbage

avocat

avocado; *vinaigrette*, with vinaigrette

avoine

oat

baba au rhum

sponge cake soaked in rum (rum baba)

baguette

long, thin loaf of white bread

baie

berry

ballotine

boned and rolled meat, poultry, fish or game, similar to a *galantine* but served hot (occasionally cold) as a main course

Banon

refreshing, slightly sharp-tasting cow's-milk cheese (sometimes made with goat and sheep milk, and sometimes marinated in *marc*), made in Provence

barbue

brill

basquaise, à la

Basque-style, with tomatoes and peppers, and often rice; garnished with *cèpes*, Bayonne ham and potatoes

bâtarde

thick butter sauce flavoured with lemon

bavarois, crème bavaroise

moulded egg yolks and whipped cream, served cold as a dessert with fruit or chocolate

bayonnaise, à la
Bayonne-style, with Bayonne ham

béarnaise
classic sauce made with egg yolks, vinegar and herbs, thickened with butter

Beaucaire
see *carré*

Beaufort
fruity cow's-milk cheese if gruyère/Emmental type, made in the Beaufort mountains (Savoie)

bécasse
woodcock

béchamel
basic white sauce made with flour, butter and milk

beignet
small sweet or savoury fritter

belle dijonnaise, à la
(in the style of the beauty from Dijon), dessert with blackcurrants

Bercy
(name denotes Paris origin), sauce for fish, made with shallots, white wine and butter

betterave
beetroot

beurre
butter; *ail*, garlic; *anchois*, with anchovy; *blanc*, sauce for fish, made with shallots cooked in white wine and vinegar, with butter whipped in; *breton*, with herbs; *d'escargots* ('snail'), seasoned butter with shallots, parsley and garlic; *maître d'hôtel* ('head waiter's'), with parsley; *marchand de vin* ('wine-merchant's'), with shallots and red wine; *de Montpellier*, with herbs, eggs, garlic and anchovies; *noir* ('black'), browned with vinegar and capers; *noix*, walnut; *noisette* ('hazelnut'), lightly browned

beurre de Gascogne
Pork dripping with garlic

bière
beer; *bouteille*, bottled; *pression*, draught

bien cuit
well cooked (of steak)

bifteck
steak (usually beef, sometimes horse), for frying or grilling; see also *saignant*, *à point*, *bleu*, *bien cuit*, *tartare*

bigarade
orange sauce, often served with duck or game

biscuit
sponge cake

bisque
thick fish soup (especially of lobster, also crayfish,

etc.) with white wine and cream

blanc

white

blanchaille

whitebait

blanquette

casserole, often of veal, with onions, mushrooms and cream sauce

blé

wheat, corn; *noir*, buckwheat

bleu

blue (of cheese); nearly raw (of steak); poached with vinegar (of trout)

Bleu d'Auvergne

cow's-milk version of Roquefort with a rich, sharp and salty taste, made in the Auvergne

Bleu de Bresse

creamy blue cow's milk cheese made in the Jura region

Bleu des Causses

cow's-milk cheese of Roquefort type, sharp, salty and rich, made in Aquitaine

boeuf

beef; *bourguignon* or (*à la*) *bourguignonne* (Burgundy-style), in red wine, with mushrooms, onions and bacon; *en daube*, stewed in red wine with bacon, salt pork and vegetables; *à la mode*, cooked in wine with vegetables and herbs, served either cold in jelly (*en gelée*) or hot

bohémienne

(Bohemian style), garnish of rice flavoured with tomatoes and fried sliced onion; cold béchamel sauce with egg yolks and vinegar

bombe (glacée)

ice-cream made in a special mould, often incorporating more than one flavour

Bondon

unripened Neufchâtel-type cheese with a fresh, slightly salty flavour and very little aroma, made in Normandy

bonne-femme

('good wife'), with white wine, mushrooms and onions (especially sole, also poultry)

bordelaise

(in the style of Bordeaux, or of the Bordelais), sauce of shallots, (red) wine and tarragon; garnish of artichokes and potatoes, or of *cèpes*, parsley, shallots and potatoes

borscht

soup of Russian origin, made with beetroot and served with soured cream

bouchée

mouthful; small pastry (with savoury filling)

boudin

large sausage; *blanc*, white sausages; *noir*, black pudding; *de Poitou*, with cream, eggs, milk, bread and spinach; *de Strasbourg*, smoked sausage made with pork, onion and bread (from Alsace region)

bouillabaisse

classic fish stew of Mediterranean coast (Provence) made with various fish and shell fish, olive oil, garlic, tomatoes and saffron

bouilleture, bouilliture

stew; *d'anguilles*, baby eels cooked in white wine with garlic, onion and egg yolks (speciality of the Poitevin marshes area)

bouillon

broth, stock, soup

boulangère

(baker's style), baked, with onions and potatoes

bouquet garni

bunch of herbs (e.g. parsley, bay and thyme) used to flavour soups and stews

bouquetière

(flower-girl's-style), artichokes, carrots, turnips, green beans, peas and cauliflower florets

bourdaloue

poached fruit in thick cream with a coating of vanilla custard and crushed macaroons, served hot; *tarte*, pear tart with custard

bourdelot

pastry encasing whole apples (speciality of Normandy)

bourguignonne

see *boeuf*

bourride

Provençal fish soup with *aïoli* (garlic mayonnaise)

Boursault

aromatic, mild but rich-flavoured cow's-milk cheese made in the Ile-de-France and Normandy

Boursin

rich, creamy cow's-milk cheese, sometimes rolled in black pepper or mixed with garlic and parsley

brandade de morue

salt cod in a purée made with oil and milk, seasoned with garlic, sometimes with truffles (speciality of Languedoc)

brebis

ewe

brème

bream; *farcie*, stuffed

bretonne
  velouté sauce with vegetables served with poultry or fish
Briand
  see *chevreuil*
Brie
  smooth, butter-textured, white cow's-milk cheese, with a full, mellow flavour, made in the Ile-de-France, Champagne, Burgundy and Lorraine; *de Coulommiers*, cream-enriched version; *de Meaux*, matured version
brioche
  bun made from rich egg dough, sometimes containing a savoury filling
brochet
  pike
brochette
  skewer; meat or fish pieces, or other food, cooked on a skewer
brocoli
  broccoli
brûlé(e)
  burnt
bruxelloise, à la
  Brussels-style; with brussels sprouts and chicory in butter; with hard-boiled yolk of egg in butter; *potage*, brussels-sprout soup
bûche
  'log', rolled sponge cake; *de Noël*, a special Christmas version

cabassol
  lamb tripe (speciality of Languedoc)
cabillaud
  fresh cod   CABRI – Kid
café
  (black) coffee; *complet*, Continental breakfast; *crème*, white; *grande crème*, large breakfast-cup of white coffee; *express*, espresso
caille
  quail; *à la vigneronne* (wine-grower-style), with grapes and *marc* (speciality of Burgundy)
Camembert
  mild, creamy cow's-milk cheese made in Normandy
canapés
  cocktail snacks; *à la bayonnaise* (Bayonne-style), pieces of bread topped with herb butter and Bayonne ham

canard

duck; *pressé*, pressed (suffocated), roasted, with the blood and juices served as a sauce (speciality of Rouen); *sauvage*, wild (e.g. mallard). See also *caneton*

cancalaise, à la

in the style of Cancale in Brittany (usually, with oysters

caneton

duckling; *d'Albuféra*, with Bayonne ham, mushrooms and madeira sauce; *à la bigarade* (or *à l'orange*), with orange sauce; *au Muscadet*, roast, with a sauce of Muscadet, shallots and cream (speciality of the Pays Nantais). See also *canard*

Cantal, (fourme de)

yellow, Cheddar-like cow's milk cheese from the Auvergne (that labelled *'haute montagne'* has the best flavour)

câpres

capers

Caprice des Dieux

small, oval-shaped, creamy cow's-milk cheese, like an enriched Brie, made in the Champagne region

carbonnade

grill or braise, theoretically over charcoal; *de boeuf* (*á la flamande*), lean beef (Flemish style), sautéed, braised with onions and beet; *de porc*, charcoal-grilled pork slices

cari

curry

carottes

carrots; *Vichy*, boiled and tossed in butter and parsley

carpe

carp; *à la bière*, cooked in beer, with soft roe; *farcie à l'alsacienne*, cooked in white wine, stuffed with other creamed fish, served with pickled cabbage and potatoes (Alsatian version of *gefüllte Fisch*); *à la juive* (Jewish style), boned, cut into sections and served cold with a sauce

carré

('square'), best end of neck (often of lamb or mutton), rack; *d'agneau Beaucaire*, roast lamb with artichokes; *de porc à la limousine* (Limousin-style), roast pork with braised cabbage and chestnuts

Carré de l'Est

white-rinded cow's-milk cheese, like a softer and milder Camembert, made in the Champagne region

cassis

blackcurrant; (*crème de*), blackcurrant liqueur

cassoulet

casserole of haricot beans, tomatoes, garlic and

different kinds of meat, especially *confit d'oie*, pork and mutton (speciality of Languedoc)

cayenne

type of pepper

céleri

celery; also abbreviated form of *céleri-rave*

céleri-rave

celeriac

cendré

('cindered'), cured in ashes: generic name for goat cheeses so treated

cèpes

boletus mushrooms; *à la bordelaise* (Bordelais-style), sautéed, with shallots and parsley

cerfeuil

chervil

cerise

cherry

cerneaux

green walnuts; *aux verjus*, marinated in grape juice, sprinkled with chervil (appetizer, speciality of Touraine)

cervelas

saveloy, pork sausage, often including pistachios and truffles; *de Lyon*, or *en brioche*, baked inside a brioche crust

cervelles

brains; usually calf's, occasionally pig's

Chabichou

conical goat's-milk cheese with full flavour and strong animal smell, made in the Poitou region

champignon

mushroom

chanterelle

small yellow mushroom shaped like a trumpet

Chantilly

see crème; also type of mayonnaise or white sauce with lemon juice and whipped cream added

charcuterie

an hors d'oeuvre of, strictly speaking, pork products, but often covers all sorts of meat productions

charcutière

(pork-butcher's style), sauce for pork, made with onions, white wine, vinegar, mustard and gherkins

charlotte

mould for desserts; hot pudding with fruit inside a bread-lined mould; *(russe)*, sponge fingers with cream or mousse and sometimes fruit

chasseur

hunter's style; garnished with mushrooms, shallots and parsley; *consommé*, game soup with port garnished with mushroom shreds; sauce with shallots, white wine, tomato and mushrooms

châtaigne

chestnut; *d'eau*, water

Châteaubriand

grilled porterhouse steak (usually for two) with a rich sauce of wine, tarragon and shallots, served with *pommes château*

châtelaine, à la

(Lady-of-the-manor style), garnish of which several versions exist, e.g. with artichoke bottoms, onion purée, madeira sauce, chestnuts, and sometimes also very small potatoes

chaude

large fruit tart (speciality of Lorraine)

chaud-froid

('hot-cold'), cold velouté sauce, for meat or poultry, made with aspic jelly, egg yolk and cream

chaudrée

fish soup of the Poitou region made with sole, plaice, eel and white wine, similar to *bouillabaisse*

chausson

turnover, made with puff pastry and usually containing a savoury filling

cheval

horse

chèvre

generic name for goat's cheese; *blanc*, firm, crumbly and sweet; *cendré*, cured in cinders to stop mould and hence with blackened outsides

chevreau

kid

chevreuil

venison, usually roe deer; *en*, cooked like venison; *sauce*, sauce for game made with vegetable stock and red wine (also, optionally, redcurrant jelly); *selle de, Briand*, saddle of, roasted, with pears in red wine

chevrotin

name for various goat's-milk cheeses

chicorée

endive; *frisée*, curly endive

chiffonade

(1) dressing for salad made with vinaigrette, beetroot, hard-boiled eggs and parsley: (2) leaf vegetables cooked with butter and served in a cream sauce

Chivry   Chippiron – Squid

velouté sauce or butter made with white wine, chervil, parsley, tarragon and chives, and shallots

chocolat

chocolate; cup of

choron

béarnaise sauce with tomato; garnish of artichokes

chou
cabbage; *cabus*, white; *farci*, stuffed; *vert*, green

choucroute
pickled cabbage, sauerkraut (speciality of Alsace); *à la strasbourgeoise* (Strasbourg-style), with pork, Strasbourg sausages and probably also thin-sliced ham

chouée
boiled, buttered cabbage of the Vendée, usually served with potatoes

chou-fleur
cauliflower; *à la polonaise* (Polish-style), boiled, coated with breadcrumbs and hard-boiled egg and fried

chou-navet
swede

chou-rave
kohl rabi

chou-rouge
red cabbage

choux
choux pastry (*pâte à chou*, type of puff pastry); *au fromage*, cheese puffs

choux brocolis
broccoli

choux de Bruxelles
brussels sprouts

choux de Chine
Chinese cabbage, Chinese leaves

ciboule
spring onion

ciboulette
chives

cidre
cider (speciality of Normandy and Britanny)

cigarette (russe)
cigarette-shaped biscuit

citron
lemon; *pressé*, fresh, squeezed juice, served as a drink with sugar

civet
rich stew; *de lièvre*, hare, casseroled with red wine and onions

clafouti(s)
flan or pancake with fruit, especially cherries

Clamart
pea soup; *à la*, garnish of peas and artichoke hearts

clou de girofle
clove

cochon
pig; *de lait*, suckling

cocotte

small ovenproof dish, especially for *oeufs en cocotte*, baked eggs (often with cream) in individual dishes; *en*, general description denoting casserole (cooked in casserole dish)

cognac

brandy, especially from the Charentes region

coeur

heart; *de boeuf, de veau*, calf's; *a la crème*, small heart-shaped cow's-milk cheese, eaten with fresh fruit, or sugar, and cream; *de filet*, finest part of beef fillet

coeurs de palmier

palm hearts: palm-tree shoots served hot or cold with vinaigrette as an appetizer

coing

quince

Colbert

see *huîtres*

colin

hake; *à la grenobloise* (Grenoble-style), cooked in butter with capers and lemon

compote

poached fresh or dried fruit served (usually cold) in its own syrup

Comté

gruyère-style cow's-milk cheese with large holes, like a stronger, fruitier Emmental; made in the Franche-Comté

concassé

crushed, chopped up or ground

concombre

cucumber

condé, (a la)

cooked fruit on rice pudding, moistened with fruit syrup

confit

(1) goose (*d'oie*), duck, turkey, pork or other meat cooked and sealed in its own fat: (2) preserved fruit (crystallized or candied)

confiture

jam

conserve

preserve of any kind, including canned meat, vegetables or fish

consommations

café fare (drinks, snacks)

consommé

clear soup; *en gelée*, served cold

coppa

corsican smoked pork sausage

coq

cock (in practice, usually a hen); *au vin*, in red wine, with mushrooms, bacon and garlic; *au vin jaune*, in white wine (yellow Arbois wine), thickened with cream and served with *morilles* (speciality of the Franche-Comté)

coquillages

shellfish

coquilles

scallop shells

coquilles St Jacques

scallops; *à la bretonne* (Breton-style), topped with breadcrumbs and baked; *flambées*, cooked in white wine, with sautéed mushrooms, flamed with cognac and finished with cream; *au vermouth*, cooked in vermouth, with white wine, cream and mushrooms

cordon bleu/rouge

(blue/red ribbon), denoting high degree of culinary skill; describing veal (*bleu*), escalope wrapped round cheese and ham; describing steak (*tournedos cordon rouge*), with ham and *foie gras*, served in a cognac sauce

cornichon

gherkin

côte

(1) rib (e.g. *de boeuf*, beef): (2) chop; *de porc à l'alsacienne* (Alsace-style), pork, served with sauerkraut, Strasbourg sausages and boiled potatoes; *de porc à la bayonnaise* (Bayonne-style), marinated pork, with *cèpes* and new potatoes; *de porc à la gasconne* (Gascony-style), marinated, served with a sauce of olives, garlic, white wine and parsley; *de porc à la vosgienne* (Vosges-style), pork, served with onion and a sauce made with white wine and mirabelle plums; *de veau Pojarski*, minced veal and bread shaped into a cutlet and fried

côtelette

cutlet; (*d'agneau*) *à la turque* (Turkish-style), sautéed lamb, served with tomato and garlic sauce and rice; (*de mouton*) *Champvallon*, mutton, baked between layers of potato and onion; *parisienne* (Paris-style), 'false cutlet' taken from rib of veal and usually slow-cooked (also known as *tendron de veau*); *de saumon Pojarski*, salmon and bread shaped into a cutlet and fried; *de volaille*, sliced chicken breast.

cotriade

white fish stew containing various types of fish and shellfish, potatoes and onions (speciality of Brittany)

cou

neck; *d'oie farci*, of (fattened) goose, stuffed with sausage meat, duck liver and truffles, served hot or cold with salad (speciality of Périgord)

Couhé-Vérac
goat's-milk cheese, wrapped in leaves, from the Poitou region

coulibiac de saumon (de volaille)
pastry filled with salmon or chicken, served hot

coulis
purée

Coulommiers
creamy white cow's-milk cheese, like a small *Brie* but with a taste closer to *Camembert*

coupe
dish or glass for desserts; ice-cream dessert, especially ice-cream and fruit (*glacée*); *Jacques*, diced, liqueur-soaked fruit, with lemon and strawberry ice-cream, sprinkled with almonds

courge
marrow, pumpkin

courgette
baby marrow, courgette

couronne
crown; *de côtelettes rôties*, crown roast of lamb

court-bouillon
stock for cooking fish, made with vegetables and either vinegar or white wine

couscous
Arab dish of steamed semolina, meat and vegetables, served with a sauce poured over

crabe
crab; *à l'anglaise* (English-style), dressed

crapiau
fruit *crêpe*, speciality of the Nivernais

craquelin
biscuit, or oval brioche from the Artois region

Crécy
with carrots; carrot soup

crème
cream; *à la*, with cream or a cream sauce; *anglaise*, egg custard; *brûlée*, 'burnt', with a brown sugar topping heated under the grill until crisp; *caramel*, vanilla custard with caramel; *Chantilly*, whipped cream with powdered sugar; *fouettée*, whipped; *glacée*, ice-; *patissière*, confectioner's custard, custard cream used in various pastries and dessert dishes

crêpe
thin, wheat-flour pancake with either sweet or savoury filling; *dentelle* ('lace'), very thin, lacy pancakes made in Brittany; *Suzette*, stuffed with sweet butter filling, Curaçao and orange juice and flamed with cognac

crevette
 prawn
croissant
 flaky, crescent-shaped roll made from a dough containing a high percentage of butter
croquant
 crunchy petit-four
croque-madame
 toasted sandwich with ham and fried egg
croque-monsieur
 toasted sandwich with gruyère cheese and ham
croquette
 food (e.g. potatoes) shaped into ovals or cylinders, covered in egg and breadcrumbs and deep-fried
croustade
 shell of pastry (otherwise rice, potato or bread) with filling
croustadine
 flaky or puff pastry case
croûte
 ('Crust'), a slice of bread or brioche, fried or baked, or a pastry covering for a piece of meat; *savoyarde*, puff pastry topped first with ham then cheese sauce and grilled
croûtons
 small cubes of fried bread, garnish for soups, stews or sometimes salad
cru
 raw
crudité
 raw vegetables served as an appetizer with a dipping sauce or mayonnaise
crustacés
 crustaceans
cuisse
 ('thigh'), frog's leg, chicken drumstick
cuisseau
 leg (of veal)
culotte
 rump (of beef)
cultivateur
 thick country soup with vegetables, bread and sometimes bacon

dard
 dace
dariole
 small pastry usually with a sweet filling such as macaroon and liqueur-flavoured cream

darne

fish steak, especially of salmon

datte

date; *de mer*, small shellfish

daube

stewed or braised meat, game, fish or poultry, but especially beef with red wine and vegetables *(boeuf en)*; *provençale*, beef with tomatoes, olives, onions and mushrooms

dauphin

see *pommes*

dauphine, à la

with a garnish of fried croquette potatoes; see also *pommes*

dauphinois

see *gratin*

DAURADE – bleam

defarde, deffarde

stew made with lamb tripe, offal and trotters (speciality of the Dauphiné)

demi-glace

('half-glaze'), rich brown sauce with a meat stock base, sometimes incorporating sherry or madeira

demoiselles de Caen/Cherbourg

scampi, cooked and served in *court-bouillon*

diable, à la

devilled, hot-flavoured; with sauce containing vinegar, herbs and *demi-glace*, perhaps also with tomatoes and shallots; or with a mustard-based sauce

diablotin

('imp'), peppered cheese toast, to accompany soup

diane

pepper sauce with cream, served with venison and steak

dieppoise, à la

Dieppe-style, cooked in white wine and garnished with shrimps and mussels (usually applies to salt-water fish)

dijonnaise, à la

Dijon-style, with mustard (occasionally, with black-currants)

dinde, dindon

turkey (hen), turkey (cock); *à la crème*, roasted with a sauce of vegetables and double cream

dindonneau

young turkey

diplomate

(1) sauce for fish, with lobster and mushrooms or truffles: (2) garnish of sweetbreads and mushrooms in madeira sauce: (3) sponge pudding, generally with chocolate and strawberries in layers, covered in

cream with vanilla, or with custard and crystallized fruit

Doria

garnish of cucumber

douillons

pear turnovers made with whole pears (speciality of Normandy)

dragée

sugared almond

Dubarry

garnish of cauliflower, with or without cheese sauce

duchesse, à la

duchess-style: (1) savoury pastry puff: (2) (potatoes), puréed, mixed with egg yolks, shaped and baked

dugléré

white wine, cream, onion and tomato sauce for poached fish

duxelles

sauce made with onion, white wine and chopped parsley; basis for sauces made with mushroom and shallot cooked in butter

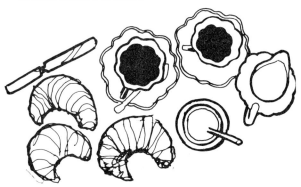

eau

water; *douce*, fresh; *gazeuse*, sparkling; *minérale*, mineral; *naturelle*, still; *potable*, drinking; *de Seltz*, soda

eau-de-vie

('water of life'), general name for spirit, especially brandy

écaille

shell (of oyster)

échalote

shallot

échine

loin, chine (of pork)

éclade (de moules)

mussels roasted over pine needles (speciality of Charentes)

éclair

long choux pastry with cream or custard filling

écrevisse

crayfish (large freshwater prawn); *gratin de queues d'*, tails, cooked in *court-bouillon*, mixed with béchamel and cream and served *au gratin* (speciality of the Dauphiné)

eglefin, egrefin

see *aiglefin*

elzekaria

Basque soup made with haricot beans, onion, cabbage and garlic

embeurré de chou

fresh boiled cabbage, pressed to dry and mixed with butter (speciality of Poitou)

émincé

thinly sliced meat covered with a sauce and re-heated

enchaud

pork terrine with garlic (speciality of Périgord)

endive

chicory

entrecôte

('between the rib'), rib steak; *béarnaise*, with béarnaise sauce; *bordelaise*, with bordelaise sauce; *Mirabeau*, grilled, topped with anchovies and served with anchovy butter and olives

épaule

shoulder (e.g. *d'agneau, de veau*)

épice

spice; *pain d'*, gingerbread

épigramme

('epigram'), either the eye of a lamb cutlet or two different cuts of lamb served together or two pieces of lamb cooked in different ways

épinards

spinach

épinée

loin, or chine (e.g. *de porc*)

escalope

veal cutlet (exceptionally, other meat or fish); *de veau Brillat-Savarin*, veal, flamed in cognac, with a cream and mushroom sauce; *de veau cordon bleu*, veal, stuffed with cheese and ham; *de veau milanaise* (Milan-style), breaded veal, sautéed and served with macaroni, tomatoes and mushrooms; *de veau normande* (Normandy-style), with calvados, cream and apple; *de veau viennoise* (Viennese), breaded veal, sautéed and served with lemon

escargots

snails; *à l'alsacienne* (Alsace-style), cooked in a

bouillon made with Alsatian wine, filled with spiced butter and *fines herbes*; *à l'arlesienne* (Arles-style), cooked in white wine with garlic, served with madeira sauce; *à la bourguignonne* (Bourgogne-style), with herbed garlic butter; *à la chablisienne* (Chablis-style), stuffed with shallots, cooked in white wine, served with herbed garlic butter; *à la vigneronne* (wine-grower's-style), fried in walnut oil, cooked in white wine with shallots and garlic

escarole
curly endive

estouffade
meat stew with wine, vegetables and herbs

estragon
tarragon

esturgeon
sturgeon

étuvée
same as *estouffade*

fagots
meatballs made with liver and fat (speciality of Charentes)

faisan
pheasant

farce
forcemeat, stuffing

farci
stuffed; *poitevin* (Poitou-style), vegetable pâté cooked in *bouillon* and served either hot or cold

farcis niçois
aubergines, tomatoes, courgettes and onions, stuffed with bits of meat, eggs, garlic and their own pulp and stewed in oil (speciality of Nice)

farçon
(1) in the Auvergne, a large pancake made with fried sausage and vegetables: (2) in the Dauphiné, a large spiced sausage: (3) in the Savoie, potatoes baked *au gratin* with milk and eggs, sometimes also including prunes and bacon

farine
flour; *d'avoine*, oatmeal; *de froment*, wheat; *de maïs*, maize; *de sarrasin*, buckwheat; *de seigle*, rye

faux-filet
'false fillet', part of beef sirloin

fechun
stuffed cabbage (speciality of the Franche-Comté)

fenouil
fennel; *tubereux*, Florence fennel
feuilletée
(filled) puff pastry
fève
broad bean
ficelle
('string'), long thin loaf; *normande* (Norman), pancake stuffed with creamed ham or mushrooms
figatelli
sausages made of pork liver (Corsican speciality)
figue
fig
filet
fillet; *de boeuf*, of beef; *mignon*, small steak
financière, à la
(financier's-style) garnished with cockscombs and kidneys; sauce made with madeira and truffles or truffle essence
fines herbes
herb mixture, including parsley, tarragon, marjoram, chives and chervil
fissurelle
small shellfish
flageolet
flageolet bean
flamande, à la
Flemish style, denoting one of several garnishes: braised cabbage, pork or sausage, carrots, turnips and boiled potatoes; red cabbage; red wine, vinegar and onions, etc
flambé
flamed, sprinkled with cognac or other spirit, and set alight
flan
open tart, sweet or savoury; *aux oignons*, onion tart, speciality of Alsace
flet
flounder
flétan
halibut
fleurs
flowers; *pralinées*, candied flower petals (speciality of Grasse)
fleurons
small crescents of puff pastry used to garnish soups and meat dishes
florentine, à la
Florence-style, served with spinach
flûte
bread roll

foie

liver; *gras*, ('fat') goose, from specially fattened birds force-fed with maize; *à l'étuvée*, braised with cognac and vegetables; *de veau à l'anglaise*, calf's, English-style, grilled with slices of bacon

foin, au

cooked in hay

fond

bottom (e.g. of artichoke)

fondu

of cheese, processed

fondu au marc, or **au raisin**

same as *tomme aux raisins*

fondue

(1) of vegetables, cooked to a pulp with butter: (2) dish (sometimes described as *au fromage*) of scrambled eggs and gruyère cheese, into which pieces of bread are dipped on skewers by the diners; *bourguignonne* ('Burgundian', though in fact of Swiss origin), pieces of tender meat, such as fillet steak, dipped on skewers in a container of boiling oil by the diners, and eaten with various sauces

fontainebleau, (à la)

(1) fresh unsalted cream cheese, rich and firm, often served as a dessert with sugar or cream: (2) (Fontainebleau-style), garnished with small heaps of *duchesse* potato filled with peas, carrots and other vegetables

forestière, à la

('forester's-style'), garnished with sautéed mushrooms, potatoes and sometimes diced bacon; also rich brown sauce made with mushrooms and flavoured with sherry

fort

strong

fouetté

whipped (of cream); whisked (of eggs)

fougeru

rich cow's-milk cheese, Coulommiers-type, of the Ile-de-France; cured in fern leaves (fern = *fougère*)

four, au

In the oven; baked or roasted

fourme

('shape'), name given to group of cheeses from south-western France, suffixed *d'Ambert* (blue-veined, slightly musty-smelling, nicknamed the French Stilton), *de Cantal*, *de Laguiole*, *de Mezenc*, *de Montbrison*, *de Pierre-sur-Haute*, *de Rochefort* and *de Salers*

foyot

béarnaise sauce with tomato

frais

cool, fresh

fraise

strawberry; *de bois* (wood), wild

framboise

raspberry

française, à la

French-style, garnished with Anna potatoes and spinach

frangipane

pastry cream with chopped almonds and macaroons, used to fill *crêpes*

frappé

iced (of desserts, drinks and fruit)

friand

small pastry with sweet or savoury filling; *de Saint-Flour*, small sausagemeat pâtés wrapped in leaves

fricandeau

(1) veal stew or braise, on a bed of chicory and sorrel: (2) in the Auvergne, pork pâté cooked in the lining of a sheep's stomach

fricassée

braised poultry or veal, previously sautéed, in cream sauce

frisée

short for *chicorée frisée*, curly endive

frit(e)

fried

frites

see *pommes*

friture

fried food in general, also small fish served fried, with lemon (e.g. *friture de la Loire*)

froid

cold

fromage

cheese; *blanc*, fresh, rather liquid cream cheese (not dissimilar to yoghurt) usually served with sugar and/or fruit; *à la crème*, cream cheese; *cuit*, cooked, cream cheese with butter and egg yolks, served hot (speciality of Lorraine); *fondu*, processed; *frais*, ('fresh'), medium-fat cheese, similar to *fromage blanc* and used in similar ways; *de tête de porc*, pig's brawn

fromage, fromaget

'fromage' means, literally, 'moulded': otherwise may denote cheesecake, speciality of Charentes

froment

wheat or wheat flour

frotée

bacon and egg tart from Lorraine, similar to a *quiche*

fruits

fruit; *confits*, crystallized; *de mer*, seafood; *rafraîchis*, salad

fumé

smoked, cured

fumée de moules

same as éclade

gâche

brioche, in western France

galantine

boned poultry, game, meat or fish, stuffed, pressed into shape, cooked in a gelatine broth and served cold

galette

(1) flat circular cake or pastry, or open tart, either savoury or sweet: (2) in Brittany, thick pancake, usually made of buckwheat flour (*farine de sarrasin*) instead of wheat flour, and often with a savoury filling (see *crêpe*)

galette de la Chaise-Dieu

strong goat's-milk cheese of the Auvergne

galicien

rich cake flavoured with pistachio nuts

galopiau, galopin

thick *crêpe* made with pieces of brioche or bread (speciality of northern France)

gamba

large prawn

gaperon d'Auvergne

soft cow's-milk (often buttermilk, *gape*) cheese flavoured with garlic

garbure

thick country vegetable soup, with a little meat or poultry cooked in it and served separately, as a piece (Gascony region)

garciaux

small eels, smoked, tossed in butter and served with cider (speciality of Brittany)

gardon

roach

garni

garnished, e.g. with vegetables

garniture

garnish, usually denoting vegetables

gâteau

elaborate cake served as a dessert; *basque*, thick tart filled with *crème patissière*; *battu*, type of brioche;

breton, large crumbly cake, or tart with apples and cherries; *de Savoie*, light sponge cake

gaudes
porridge made with oats, buckwheat or maize flour, according to region, and enriched with cream, served either hot or cold and sliced (speciality of Burgundy and Franche-Comté)

gaufre
waffle

gelée
jelly

gendarme
smoked herring

genièvre, baies de
juniper berries

genoese, genoise
sponge cake filled with chocolate or fruits

germiny
soup made with cream, sorrel and egg yolk

gibier
game; *d'eau*, wild water fowl; *de plume*, feathered (birds)

gigorit
pig's head stewed in wine and its own blood (Poitou region)

gigot
leg (of lamb or mutton)

gigue
haunch of venison (or wild boar)

glaçage
icing

glace
ice-cream; *au café*, coffee; *au chocolat*, chocolate

glacé
frozen; iced (of cake); glazed

gogues
rustic meat pudding with herbs made in the Anjou region

gougère
choux pastry encasing a creamy egg-and-gruyère filling

goujon
strip (of sole), fried

grand veneur
('great hunter'), sauce with vegetable stock, vinegar, currant jelly and cream

granité
Italian water ice, slightly sweetened with sugar

gras-double
tripe; *à la lyonnaise* (Lyon-style), with onions and parsley

gratin, gratiné
encrusted, usually with breadcrumbs and/or a hard grating cheese

gratin dauphinois
sliced potatoes baked with milk and cream and often also grated gruyère

grenade
pomegranate

grenouilles
frogs; *frites*, deep-fried legs; *à la mode de Boulay*, breaded legs baked with shallots, lemon and parsley; *à la luçonnaise*, Luçon-style, fried frog's legs, previously marinated in vinegar, with garlic (speciality of the Poitou region)

gribiche
(1) cold herbed sauce with hard-boiled egg yolks, oil and vinegar: (2) mayonnaise containing chopped hard-boiled eggs, capers, herbs and pickles

grillade
grilled dish or toasted sandwich; *au fenouil*, with fennel (fish grilled on leaves)

grillé
grilled or toasted

grillons
goose or pork scraps that remain after cooking *confits* (speciality of Périgord)

griset
black bream (sea fish)

grive
thrush, often as a *terrine*

groseille
redcurrant; *à maquereau*, gooseberry

grondin
gurnard (sea fish)

gruyère
generic name for Emmental and similar cheeses

guenilles
('rags'), fritters (speciality of the Auvergne)

haché
chopped

hachis
minced meat, often served in a sauce; *parmentier*, shepherd's pie

hachua
Basque stew made with Bayonne ham, veal or beef, onions and peppercorns

halicot (or **haricot**) **de mouton**
(Irish-type) mutton stew

hareng
herring; *blanc* (or *salé*), salt; *fumé*, smoked, served cold; *mariné à la fécampoise*, Fécamp style, marinated, preserved with boiling vinegar and wine with lemon slices and vegetables, and served cold; *roulé*, rollmop; *à la quimperlaise*, Quimper-style, grilled, and served with a mustard sauce

haricots
haricot beans; *blancs à la bretonne* (Brittany-style), with onions browned in butter, tomatoes and garlic; *blanc frais*, fresh; *blanc secs*, dried; *d'Espagne* (Spanish), runner; *verts*, green (French)

hochepot
thick soup of Flemish origin with bits of pig meat, salt pork, beef and mutton, cabbage and various root vegetables

hollandaise
light béarnaise sauce without shallots or tarragon, but with lemon juice

homard
lobster; *à l'armoricaine* (*à l'americaine*), Breton-style (American-style), cooked in oil, with tomatoes and shallots; *à la parisienne*, Paris-style, meat served (cold) in the shell with mayonnaise; *Newburg*, pieces, with cognac, sherry or madeira and cream; *Thermidor*, split in two, cooked *au gratin* flavoured with mustard and served with a wine sauce

hongroise, à la
Hungarian-style, with paprika and usually also tomatoes and onions, often with a soured cream sauce

huile
oil

huîtres
oysters; *à la bordelaise*, Bordelais-style, with sausage; *Colbert*, fried; *en écaille*, in the shell; *à la Monselet*, threaded on skewers and fried; *villeroi*, coated with white sauce, egg and breadcrumbs and deep-fried

hure (de porc, de sanglier)
(pig's, wild boar's) head, usually served as jellied brawn; *blanche*, Alsatian sausage made with pig's head and ham knuckle; *de porc à la parisienne*, pig tongues, Paris-style, in aspic

ile flottante
(1) caramelized *oeufs à la neige* served with almonds:

(2) sponge cake soaked in kirsch, layered with preserve, covered with whipped cream and floated in vanilla custard

imbrucciate
Corsican white cheese tart

impératrice, à l'
(Empress-style), rice-based dessert or cake

jambon
ham; *à la bayonnaise* (Bayonne-style), cooked in madeira with tomatoes, mushrooms, sausage and rice; *de Bayonne*, smoked Bayonne ham; *braisé à la lie de vin*, boiled, then braised in the lees of red wine with herbs and vegetables (speciality of Burgundy); *cru*, raw (usually salted and smoked); *de Parme* (from Parma in Italy), very thinly sliced raw ham; *persillé*, with parsley, cooked in white wine and served cold in aspic (Burgundy speciality for Easter)

jardinière, à la
(in the style of the gardener's wife), with diced mixed vegetables

jésus (de morteau)
large smoked pork liver sausage, speciality of Franche-Comté region, with a peg at one end showing that it has been smoked, over juniper and pine wood

Joinville
(1) sauce for fish, with egg yolk, cream and purées of crayfish and shrimp, sometimes with diced truffle: (2) boned chicken, stuffed with cream, egg whites, sweetbreads and truffles and casseroled, served with a sauce of the juices, verbena liqueur and brandy

julienne
(1) vegetable consommé: (2) shreds or delicate strips of vegetables or other food

jus
juice; *de fruits*, fruit

Kiev, à la
Kiev-style; *poulet*, deep-fried boned breasts encasing herb butter

kirsch
spirit made with wild cherries, often used in fruit desserts

lait
milk

laitance, laite
soft roe (of fish)

laitue
lettuce; *romaine*, cos

langouste
spiny lobster, crayfish, usually served boiled or stewed; *à la calvaise* (Calvi-style), in a highly spiced tomato sauce; *à la parisienne*, Paris-style, served cold with mayonnaise; *Newburg*, sautéed with cognac, madeira and cream; *Thermidor*, cooked in the shell with wine sauce

langoustine
large prawns, scampi

langue
tongue; *de boeuf*, ox; *de chat* (cat's tongue), long, thin, crisp biscuit

languedocienne, à la
Languedoc-style, with garlic, sometimes also with tomatoes, aubergines or *cèpes*

lapereau
baby rabbit; *en blanquette*, stewed

lapin
rabbit; *à la flamande* (Flanders-style) marinated in red wine, braised with prunes and olives; *aux pruneaux*, with prunes; *aux raisins*, with grapes

lard
bacon or pork fat; *de poitrine*, salted or smoked belly of pork

lardon
rasher or strip (of bacon or pork fat)

laurier
bay (leaves)

lentilles
lentils

levraut
leveret (young hare)

liègoise, à la
Liège-style; with juniper berries, or sometimes gin

lièvre
hare; *à la broche* (Bourbonnais), marinated and cooked on the spit; *(farci) en cabessal (chabessal)*, stuffed with highly spiced mixture of veal, pork and ham, shallots and garlic, and cooked in wine (originally from Limousin); *à la périgourdine* or *à la royale* (Périgord-style, royal style), stuffed with *foie gras* and truffles, cooked in wine and *cognac* (originally from Limousin)

limon
lime

LIMANDE - lemon sole

limousine, à la
Limousin-style, accompanied by braised red cabbage and chestnuts
lit
bed (e.g. *lit d'oignons*)
livarot
spicy, pungent, cow's-milk cheese from Normandy
livèche
lovage
lompe
lumpfish
lonzo
dried and salted raw ham, made from pork fillet (speciality of Corsica)
lorette
with asparagus, chicken croquettes and truffles
lorraine
Lorraine-style; *oeufs à la*, eggs baked with bacon, cream and cheese; see also *quiche*
lotte
Loup - Bass
monkfish; *à la marseillaise*, Marseille-style, cooked with cheese, tomato and saffron
lyonnaise
Lyon-style, with onions; see *pommes de terre*

macaire
see *pommes de terre*
macaron
macaroon
macédoine (de fruits, de legumes)
('miscellany'), mixture of fruit or vegetables, raw or cooked, served hot or cold (fresh fruit salad, in its own juice, vegetables with mayonnaise or dressing)
madeleine
small fluted sponge-cake, originally from Lorraine

madère

madeira

madrilene, à la

Madrid-style, tomato-flavoured; *consommé*, clear chicken broth flavoured with tomato juice and usually also peppers and celery

magret, maigret

breast fillet of fattened duck, usually lightly grilled or fried

maigre

thin, lean, low-fat

maillot, à la

mixed vegetable garnish including carrots, turnips, glazed onions, braised lettuce, French beans and peas, usually served with ham

maïs

maize, sweetcorn

maison

house; *à la, de la*, homemade, house speciality

maître d'hôtel

see *beurre*

malouine, à la

Saint-Malo-style

maltaise

Maltese-style, with oranges; *Hollandaise* sauce made with zest and juice of blood orange

mange-tout

('eat-all'), sugar pea, the pod of which is eaten in addition to the 'peas' inside

maquereau

mackerel; *aigre-doux*, sweet and sour, simmered with vinegar, sugar and vegetables; *à la façon de quimper*, served cold with egg and herb sauce; *grillé*, grilled; *maître d'hôtel*, sautéed in butter, sprinkled with lemon juice.

marc

spirit distilled from grape residue

marcassin

young boar; *à la Saint-Hubert*, roast cutlets with mushrooms

maréchale, à la

garnished with asparagus tips and truffles

marée

fresh seafood

Marengo

cooked in white wine with tomatoes and herbs; see also *poulet, veau*

mariné

marinated; pickled

marinière, à la

mariner's-style, cooked in white wine, with shallots

and herbs (especially mussels)

marinoun
very large sausage (speciality of Languedoc)

marjolaine
marjoram

marmande
type of tomato

marmelade
purée of fruit; *en*, cooked to a pulp

marmite
large cooking pot used, e.g. for *pot-au-feu*; stew cooked in it; *bressane*, Bresse-style, poached chicken; *dieppoise*, Dieppe-style, fish stew with vegetables, wine and cream

maroilles
strong, reddish-rinded, cream-coloured cow's-milk cheese made in northern France

marron
chestnut; *glacé*, preserved, glazed and sweet

massepain
marzipan

matelote
rich mixed fish stew, usually with wine; sauce made with fish stock and wine

mayonnaise
dressing made with egg yolk and oil, served cold

médaillon
medallion, round cut of meat (see *noisette* and *tournedos*) or other food

Melba
see *pêche*

melon
melon; *au porto*, chilled and served with port

menouille
salt pork, served with potatoes, beans and onions

menthe
mint   HERGUEZ- Spicy Sausage

meringue
stiffly beaten egg whites and sugar, baked in a low oven until crisp, served with cream and sometimes fruit

merlan
whiting; *en colère* ('angry'), fried, presented with its tail in its mouth; *à la française* (French-style), fillets fried and served with tomato sauce

merlu
hake; *à la koskera* (Basque speciality), cooked with asparagus, peas, garlic and potatoes

meunière
(Miller's-style), of fish, coated with flour, fried in butter, served with the pan juices

meurette
sauce with red wine and butter, served with fresh-water fish and poached eggs

mi-chèvre
general name for cheese made of half (minimum 25%) goat's, half cow's milk (or cream), producing a light, rich, aromatic result

miel
honey

milanaise, à la
Milan-style, with an egg-and-breadcrumb coating, served with parmesan cheese

mille-feuille
('thousand leaves'), puff pastry layered with jam and cream or (less usually) with savoury items

Mirabeau, à la
with anchovies

mirabelle
small yellow plum

mirepoix
diced vegetables cooked in butter as a base for sauces and stews

miroton
stew made with cooked meat and onions

mode (de), à la
in the style (of)

moka
mocha, coffee-flavoured

monsieur, fromage de or **Monsieur-Fromage**
(Mr Cheese), fruity cow's-milk cheese made in Normandy, of similar type to Brie though richer and stronger

Mont Blanc
sweet dish made with chestnut purée and cream

Montmorency, à la
with cherries

mornay
béchamel sauce with grated cheese

morue
dry salt cod, also known as stockfish; *à la languedocienne*, Languedoc-style, cooked with potatoes and garlic until completely combined

mouclade
mussels, with cream, egg yolks and white wine

moules
mussels; *à l'armoricaine*, Brittany-style, with onions and tomatoes; *barbues* ('bearded'), larger type of mussel; *à la camarguaise*, Camargue-style, with white wine and lemon mayonnaise; *marinière*, mariner's-style, cooked unshelled with white wine, shallots and parsley; *poulette*, with *sauce poulette*

mousse
mousse, frothy sweet or savoury egg mixture; *au chocolat*, chocolate; *au citron*, lemon
mousseline
hollandaise sauce lightened with whipped cream or egg-whites; *pommes de terre*, potatoes creamed with milk and butter
mousseuse
sauce made with butter, lemon juice and egg yolks
mousseux
sparkling (of wine)
moutarde
mustard
mouton
mutton, sheep; *à la bretonne*, Brittany-style, braised and served with haricots
mûre
blackberry
mulet
grey mullet
Munster, Münster
strong, spicy, smelly cheese made in Alsace
muscle
Provençal name for mussel
mye
type of clam, found particularly on the Atlantic coast
myrtille
bilberry

nage, à la
('swimming'), cooked in an aromatic *court-bouillon*
Nantua
Nantua-style, with crayfish; *sauce*, cream sauce with crayfish and butter.
Navarin
lamb or mutton stew with small onions, potatoes and other vegetables, sometimes called *à la printanière*
navet
turnips
nesselrode
ice-cream into which are beaten puréed chestnuts and, optionally, candied fruit and liqueur
Neufchâtel
soft, white, cow's-milk cheese made in Normandy, medium-to-strong in flavour according to age
Newburg
see *homard*

niçoise
Nice-style, generally with tomatoes, garlic, olives and capers, sometimes also anchovies, French beans and/or artichokes

nivernaise, à la
Nivernais-style, with turnips and carrots

noisettes
hazelnuts; also, small, tender pieces of rib or loin

noix
nuts, walnuts

normande, à la
Normandy-style, with cream, or apples, or calvados, or cider; *sauce*, made with white wine and cream, to accompany fish.

nougat
chewy sweet made with roasted almonds and honey

oeufs
eggs; *à l'auvergnate*, Auvergne-style, poached, served on cabbage with fried sausage; *brouillés*, scrambled, *à la périgourdine* or *Rossini*, with truffles and *foie gras*; *en cocotte*, baked in ramekins (small ovenproof dishes), sometimes with cream; *à la coque*, soft-boiled; *durs*, hard-boiled; *farcis*, stuffed; *au four*, baked; *frits*, fried, *à la bayonnaise*, with Bayonne ham, *à la languedocienne*, Languedoc-style, with fried aubergine and a garlic-and-tomato sauce; *à la neige* (snow eggs), small mounds of beaten egg white poached in milk and served with vanilla custard (see also *île flottante*); *pochés*, poached; *à la poêle*, fried

oignons
onions

oie
goose, *à l'alsacienne*, Alsace-style, stuffed with sausage, roasted, served with pickled cabbage (sauerkraut), Strasbourg sausages and pork; *à la flamande*, Flanders-style, stuffed, braised and garnished with vegetables; see also *confit*

olive
olive

omelette
fluffy pancake made of beaten eggs fried in butter; *aux fines herbes*, with finely chopped parsley, tarragon, chervil and chives; *norvégienne* (Norwegian), sweet soufflèed omelette filled with ice-cream

orange
orange

origan
  oregano
Orloff
  with onion sauce and cheese
os
  bone
oseille
  sorrel
oursins
  sea urchins

pain
  bread; *bis*, brown; *complet*, wholemeal; *d'épice*, gingerbread; *grillé*, toast, *gros*, large, crusty loaf; *petit*, roll; *de seigle*, rye
palmiers
  small heart-shaped pastry puffs
palombe
  wild pigeon
palourdes
  clams; *farcies*, stuffed with shallots, cream and cheese, speciality of Brittany
pamplemousse
  grapefruit
panais
  parsnip
pané (à)
  coated (with)
pannequet
  small rolled *crêpe* filled with jam
parfait
  ice-cream made with eggs and whipped cream, with a flavouring
parisienne
  Paris-style, with potatoes and leeks or other vegetables
parmentier
  generally denotes potatoes; *hachis*, with minced meat, like shepherd's pie; *potage*, soup made with potatoes and leeks; see also *pommes de terre*
pâte
  pastry, cake
pâté
  (1) meat or fish paste; *de campagne*, of the country-side, coarse-textured, usually made with pork; *de foie gras*, of goose liver from force-fed birds; *maison*, of the house, homemade, smooth-textured meat pâté: (2) pie or pastry, sweet or savoury

patissière
  pastry-cook; *crème*, confectioner's custard, custard
  cream used in various dessert dishes

paupiettes
  thin slices of meat wrapped round a savoury filling to
  form cork-sized rolls, as for a beef olive

pauvre homme
  ('poor man'), sauce with onions, vinegar, mustard
  and tomato

pavé
  ('paving-stone') (1) thick slice of beef steak; (2)
  mousse or purée, served cold set in a mould

pavé (d'Auge, de Moyaux)
  spicy, firm-textured cheese made in Normandy

paysanne
  ('peasant-' or country-style) meat or poultry, usually
  braised, and garnished with sliced, lightly cooked
  carrots and turnips, plus onions, bacon and potatoes

pebronata
  spicy Corsican beef stew

pêche
  peach; *Melba*, served with ice-cream and raspberry
  sauce

perdreau
  partridge

périgourdine, à la
  (Périgord-style), with truffles and sometimes also
  foie gras

périgueux
  (after the capital of Périgord), sauce with truffle
  essence

persane, à la
  Persian-style; *côtelette*, with aubergines, sweet
  peppers and tomatoes; *sole*, with sweet peppers,
  rice, lobster sauce and paprika

persil
  parsley

petite marmite
  clear meat soup served in individual earthenware
  dish or *marmite*

petit four
  ('little oven'), small biscuit or sweet, flavoured with
  almond, chocolate, etc. and served at the end of the
  meal

petit pain
  (bread) roll

petit salé
  salt pork

petits pois
  small, young peas

Petit-Suisse

fresh, cream-enriched, unsalted cheese made throughout France and marketed in small, cylindrical containers; eaten with sugar or fruit

pièce de boeuf

top rump of beef

pieds

feet; -de-cheval ('horses' hooves'), type of oyster; de porc, pigs' trotters; de mouton, sheep's

piemontaise, à la

Piedmont-style, with mushroom (formerly truffle) risotto

pigeon

pigeon; en crapaudine, flattened slightly and grilled

pilaf, pilau, pilaw

pilau (flavoured) rice

pilon

drumstick (poultry)

piment

pimento, sweet red or green pepper, capsicum

pintade

guinea-fowl

pipérade

lightly scrambled eggs with fried tomatoes, peppers, onions and basil, often served with Bayonne ham (Basque speciality)

piquante

sauce with shallots, white wine, vinegar, pickles and herbs

pirojki

small croquettes filled with cheese or minced game, fish or vegetables (of Russian origin)

pissaladière

tart with onions, black olives, anchovies and often tomatoes (speciality of Nice)

pistache

pistachio nut

plateau

platter, tray, large plate (e.g. for seafood or cheeses)

plombières

ice-cream with vanilla, kirsch, candied fruit and crème Chantilly; or almond ice-cream with apricot jam

pluvier

plover

pochouse

stew made with freshwater fish, especially eel, cooked with white wine (speciality of Bourgogne)

point, à

(of steak), medium rare; (of fruit or cheese), just ripe or ready to eat

pointe

tip (e.g. of asparagus)

poire

pears; *belle dijonnaise*, poached and served with blackcurrant ice-cream and sauce; *belle-Hélène*, poached, served with vanilla ice-cream and topped with a hot chocolate sauce; *vigneronne*, or *au vin rouge*, in red wine

poireaux

leeks; à la niçoise (Nice-style), cooked in oil, with tomatoes and garlic

pois

pea(s); *cassés*, split; *chiche*, chick-pea; *princesse*, mange-touts

poisson

fish

poitrine

breast; *d'agneau*, lamb; *de boeuf*, brisket of beef; *de porc*, belly of pork

poivrade

game sauce made with meat juices, pepper and vinegar

poivre

pepper; *blanc*, white; *de Cayenne*, cayenne; *gris* or *noir*, black; *vert*, green peppercorns

poivre d'Auvergne

black-coated cheese of the *tomme* family, moderately flavoured with black pepper

poivron

capsicum, sweet red or green pepper

pojarski

cutlet assembled from chopped meat or fish and fried

polonaise

Polish-style, with a garnish of sieved hard-boiled egg yolks and breadcrumbs in butter

pommes

apples

pommes (de terre)

potatoes; *allumettes*, matchsticks, fried; *à l'anglaise*, English-style, peeled and boiled; *Anna*, pancake of layered slices of potato, fried; *à la basquaise*, Basque-style, hollowed out and filled with tomato, pimentos and ham, baked with a breadcrumb topping; *boulangère* (baker's-style), cooked with onions in butter and baked with onions; *château*, whole, small oval potatoes sautéed in butter; *dauphin*, grated and cooked as pancakes; *dauphine*, small croquettes of creamed potato, breaded and fried; *duchesse*, puréed with egg yolks, glazed and browned in the oven; *frites*, fried (chips); *frites chip*, game chips; *impériale*, baked in their skins with butter, cream and mushrooms; *lyonnaise*, sliced and sautéed with onions; *macaire*, mashed with butter, shaped and baked; *mousseline*, mashed, with whipped cream; *noisette*, as pommes château with smaller potatoes the size of large hazelnuts; *à la normande*, cooked with onions and leeks in butter and browned; *paille*, sliced like straw (*paille*) and fried; *à la parisienne*, small, rolled in meat jelly; *parmentier*, diced and cooked in butter; *Pont-Neuf*, fried (chips); *en robe de chambre* (in a dressing-gown) or *en robe des champs* (in field garb), boiled, steamed or baked unpeeled; *sarladaise* (from Sarlat in Périgord), sliced, cooked in the oven with goose fat and sometimes truffles; *savoyarde*, as *boulangère*, with the addition of bacon and a topping of grated cheese

porc
pork; *carré de porc à la périgourdine*, cold boned loin, braised in wine with truffles; *côtes de porc à l'ardennaise* (Ardennes-style), pork chops with juniper berries; *noisettes de, aux pruneaux*, thick pieces of pork cooked with prunes served with a rich red-currant sauce (Touraine speciality)

Pont-l'Evèque
sweet-flavoured, tangy, strong-smelling cow's-milk cheese from Normandy

porcelet
sucking pig

Port (de) Salut
mild cow's-milk cheese made throughout France (variety of Saint-Paulin)

portugaise
(Portuguese), with tomatoes cooked with garlic and onions

(petit) pot-au-crème, de chocolat
light dessert, served in small individual dishes, of cream mixed with egg yolks and various flavourings

potage
thick country soup

pot-au-feu
('pot on the fire'), classic two-course dish, beef broth followed by boiled beef and fresh vegetables, e.g. onions, carrots, leeks and turnips (many regional variants, including substitution of poultry for meat); *à la carcassonne*, Carcassonne-style, with, in addition, bacon, stuffed cabbage and haricots; *à la languedocienne*, Languedoc-style, with, in addition, salt pork

potée
mixed vegetable and meat soup; *auvergnate*

(Auvergne-style), with beans, pig's head, *cervelas*, pork belly or salt pork, cabbage, potatoes and various other vegetables, poured over dried bread; *bretonne* (Brittany-style), with pork, sausage, cabbage and carrot

pouding

(substantial) pudding (not any dessert dish)

poularde

pullet; *au blanc*, poached, with cream sauce; *demi-deuil* (half-mourning), studded with truffles and poached; *Tosca*, pot-roasted with fennel

poule

hen; *au pot*, stuffed and poached, with vegetables

poule de mer

John Dory

poulet

chicken; *à l'alsacienne*, Alsace-style, with noodles, peas and parmesan cheese; *basquaise*, Basque-style, casseroled with tomatoes, peppers, mushrooms and peppercorns; *à la bohemienne* (Bohemian-style), with mushrooms, artichokes and herbs; *Carmen*, boned roast, with a mayonnaise sauce incorporating red peppers, peas, mustard and rice; *à l'estragon*, poached, with tarragon; *en gelée*, in aspic; *(à la) Kiev*, boned breasts deep-fried with herb or garlic butter inside; *Marengo*, sautéed with tomatoes, garlic and mushrooms (and, theoretically, fried egg, crayfish tails and croûtons); *(sauté) à la provençale*, Provence-style, fried with tomatoes, onions, garlic, white wine, served with olives, mushrooms and anchovies; *vallée d'Auge*, with cream and tiny onions

poulette

(1) pullet, young chicken; (2) *velouté* sauce with lemon juice, parsley and sometimes mushrooms

pousse-café

short-drink (spirit) taken after coffee

poussin

very young, small chicken, usually served as an individual portion

poutassou

blue whiting

praline

praline, mixture of toasted ground nuts, usually almonds, and sugar, added to dessert dishes

pressé

pressed; *citron*, freshly squeezed lemon juice

pression

('pressure'), draught (beer)

primeurs

first, or early, vegetables

princesse, à la

('Princess-style), garnished with asparagus tips, artichoke and small potatoes

printanier (printanière, à la)

('Spring-style'), diced carrots or turnips, blanched, with peas and French beans; see also *Navarin*

profiteroles

profiteroles, small balls or fingers of choux pastry filled with custard or whipped cream, covered with chocolate (*au chocolat*) or other sauce

provençale, à la

with tomato, and usually garlic and onions

prune

plum; *de Damas*, damson

pruneau

prune

puits d'amour

('well of love'), small pastry with sweet filling of fruit or cream

purée

purée; *argenteuil*, asparagus; *Crécy*, carrots; *parmentier*, potatoes; *de pommes de terre*, mashed potatoes; *Rachel*, artichoke hearts; *Saint-Germain*, peas or split peas; *soubise*, onions; *Vichy*, carrots

quenelles

small poached sausage-shaped mousses; *de brochet*, pike; *de volaille*, chicken

queue

tail; *de boeuf*, ox; *d'écrevisse*, crayfish

quiche

open tart with savoury filling; *lorraine*, Lorraine-style, with eggs, cream and bacon

râble

saddle (of hare or rabbit); *de lapin à la moutarde*, speciality of Dijon, rabbit roasted with mustard and served with cream in the sauce

ragoût

stew

raie

skate; *au beurre noir*, with black butter

raifort

horseradish

raisin

grape; *de Corinthe*, currant; *de sec*, raisin; *de Smyrne*, sultana

ramier

wood-pigeon

râpé

grated (cheese)

ratatouille

vegetables, such as aubergines, courgettes, tomatoes, peppers, onions and garlic, cooked in oil and served either hot or cold

ravigote

(from the verb *ravigoter*, to enliven), type of vinaigrette with mustard, capers, gherkins, onion, lemon juice and herbs, served cold

Reblochon

smooth, sweet, creamy cow's-milk cheese from the Savoie

reine-claude

greengage

rémoulade

mayonnaise with capers, onions, gherkins and herbs

rhubarbe

rhubarb

rhum

rum

rillette

minced pork cooked in fat (speciality of Touraine)

rillon

pieces of pork or goose cooked in fat

ris

sweetbreads (calf's or lamb's); *Régence*, calf's braised, with a sauce containing cream, *foie gras*, mushrooms and port

rissole

small deep-fried pastry puff with savoury filling

riz

rice; *à l'impératrice*, with custard, crystallized fruit and cream, in a mould; *à l'indienne*, Indian-style, boiled; *pilaf*, pilaw, browned in butter with chopped onions

Robert
sauce, often served with chops, made with onions, white wine, vinegar and mustard

rognons
kidneys; *Beaugé*, in Bordeaux, with madeira and mustard; *vert pré* (green meadow), grilled with butter and parsley, garnished with watercress

rognons de coq
kidney beans

Roquefort
sharp, salty sheep's-milk cheese, blue, with a buttery texture; made on the Causse plateau

Rossini
see *tournedos*

rôti
roast; the meat course; *de porc Montmorency*, pork, with a wine and cherry sauce

rouge
red

rouget
mullet; *à la niçoise*, Nice-style, with tomatoes, anchovies and black olives

roulade
roll of meat, fish or other food, sometimes stuffed

roulé
rolled

royale
coated in cream sauce, with truffles; *consommé*, clear soup with shaped pieces of savoury custard as garnish

rutabaga
swede

sabayon
('*zabaglione*'), sauce of eggs yolks and sugar with wine or liqueur, served warm

safran
saffron

saignant
underdone, rare (of steak)

Saint-Germain
purée of peas or split peas (sometimes also with artichokes)

Saint-Hubert
game consommé with white wine

Saint-Marcellin
mild-flavoured cow's-milk cheese (formerly made from goat's milk) of the Dauphiné

Sainte-Maure

strong-flavoured, soft goat's-milk cheese produced in the Touraine in long cylinders

Saint-Michel

coffee sponge cake

Saint-Nectaire

firm-textured, fruity-flavoured cow's-milk cheese from the Auvergne, sometimes stirred into soup

Saint-Paulin

mild cow's-milk cheese, made throughout France

salade

salad; *folle* ('foolish': *nouvelle cuisine* term), green beans, *foie gras* and shellfish; *Francillon*, mussels, potatoes marinated in Chablis, truffles, hot vinaigrette; *Lorette*, lamb's lettuce, beetroot and celery; *mimosa*, lettuce with orange and hard-boiled egg; *monégasque* (Monaco-style), with tiny fish, tomatoes and rice; *niçoise* (Nice-style), with tomatoes, olives, capers, tuna, hard-boiled eggs and green peppers (many variants exist); *panachée*, mixed; *russe*, (Russian), various vegetables, diced, with mayonnaise; *tiede*, warm; *verte*, green; *Waldorf*, celery, apple and walnut

salé

salt, salted

salpicon

pieces of meat or fish with diced vegetables in sauce, used as a stuffing or garnish

sandre   SANGWER — Wild Boar

fresh-water fish of the Loire

santé

('health'), with potatoes and sorrel

sarrasin

buckwheat

sauce

sauce

saucisse

sausage (type that must be cooked)

saucisson

sausage, dried or cooked type

sauge

sage

saumon

salmon; *blanc*, hake

sauté

('jumped'), sautéed, or tossed in butter, fried

savarin

ring-shaped sponge cake, soaked in syrup and liqueur or spirit

savoyarde, à la

(Savoie-style), usually, with potatoes, eggs, cream and gruyère cheese

scarole
batavian endive
seigle
rye
sel
salt
selle
saddle; *d'agneau*, of lamb; *de chevreuil*, of venison; *de veau*, of veal
semoule
semolina; *gâteau de*, pudding, oven-baked and with a jam sauce poured over it
sirop
syrup, juice
soissonaise
Soissons-style, with haricots
sole
sole; *bonne-femme* ('good wife'), poached in white wine with mushrooms and served with potato; *cardinal*, poached, with a cream and crayfish sauce; *dugléré*, poached with a white wine, cream, tomato, parsley and onion sauce; *marguéry*, with white wine, mussels and prawns; *meunière*, coated with flour, fried in butter, served with the pan juices, parsley and lemon; *véronique*, poached in white wine, with grapes to garnish
sorbet
water ice, usually fruit-flavoured
soubise
béchamel sauce with onion
soufflé
('puffed'), soufflé, light, frothy dish, sweet or savoury, made with eggs and oven-baked; *à l'orange*, orange
soupe
soup; *à la bière*, with beer (speciality of Alsace)
spätzel
noodles made with eggs (in Alsace)
spetzli
rich dumplings, speciality of Alsace, served with butter
spoom
water ice, flavoured with wine or fruit juice and mixed with meringue
Stanley
with a smooth curry sauce
steack, steak
steak; *au poivre*, pepper steak, covered in crushed peppercorns, fried and flambéed in cognac
sucre
sugar

sultane, à la

garnished with red cabbage and *duchesse* potatoes

suprême

(1) breast of chicken; *à la crème*, sautéed, served with a cognac and cream sauce: (2) reduced velouté sauce with cream

tapenade

anchovy paste or purée with capers, black olives and tuna

tartare

(1) mayonnaise with onions, capers, mustard and chopped chives: (2) steak, raw, minced, and mixed with egg and onion

tarte

tart, with sweet or savoury filling; *alsacienne aux abricots*, apricot pie; *au citron*, lemon tart; *aux fraises*, strawberry tart; *Tatin*, with apples, upside down, caramelised, served hot

tartelette

small individual tart

tendrons

strips of breast of veal, also known as *côtelettes parisiennes*

terrine

coarse-textured pâté; also the dish in which it is cooked

tête

head; *de veau*, calf's, often set in aspic, alternatively *en tortue* (see below)

thon

tuna or tunny fish

thym

thyme

timbale (de)

cooked in a mould called a *timbale*

tomates

tomatoes; *à la provençale*, halved and baked with a sprinkling of parsley and garlic

tomme

family of cheeses produced mainly in Alpine areas, usually from goat's or sheep's milk, and generally smooth in texture and mild in flavour; *aux raisins*, steeped in *marc* (also known as *fondu aux raisins*)

topinambour

Jerusalem artichoke

tortoni

ice-cream dessert flavoured with rum and almonds

tortue
turtle; *en*, in a sauce containing herbs, tomato and
madeira; or a soup made with beef stock and pieces
of turtle
tournedos
thick slices of beef fillet; *cordon rouge*, sautéed with
ham and *foie gras*, with a rich port and brandy sauce;
à la monégasque, Monaco-style, sautéed, with
aubergines, black olives and tomato sauce; *Rossini*,
with a sauce of truffles, *foie gras* and madeira
tourte
(1) pie, tart; *de truffes à la périgourdine*, hot pie filled
with truffles and *foie gras* soaked in cognac: (2)
round loaf of bread
tripes
tripe; *à la mode de Caen*, cooked in cider and
calvados, with trotters, vegetables and herbs; *à la
niçoise*, Nice-style, beef tripe with vegetables and
garlic; pork and beef tripe in tomato sauce
truffes
truffles; *sous la cendre*, wrapped in oiled paper or tin-
foil and cooked under ashes, or wrapped in dough and
baked; or wrapped in a thin slice of fresh bacon and
oiled paper and cooked under ashes
truite
trout; *au bleu*, boiled live in water with vinegar,
which makes it turn blue; *meunière*, dipped in flour
and sautèed in butter, with parsley and lemon

vacherin
ice-cream in a meringue shell
Vallée d'Auge
sauce with calvados and cream
veau
veal; *ballotine de*, boned, stuffed and braised shoulder;
brochettes de, grilled skewered veal cubes; *Marengo*,
sautéed, in oil with tomatoes, onions and mushrooms; *poitrine de, aux groseilles, vertes*, breast,
braised with a sauce of white wine and gooseberries
velouté
('velvety'), classic sauce made with white stock and
wine; *Yvonne*, cream of chicken soup which includes
lettuce
venaison
venison; see also *chevreuil*
véronique, à la
with white grapes

verte
green; *sauce*, mayonnaise with herbs (parsley, tarragon and chervil)
Vichy, à la
carrots cooked in Vichy water
viennoise, à la
Vienna-style, with capers, parsley, chopped hard-boiled eggs, olives, lemon and butter
villeroi, à la
coated with thick mushroom-flavoured *sauce allemande*, egg and breadcrumbs, and fried
vinaigre
vinegar
vinaigrette
dressing for cold food, made with oil, wine vinegar and seasoning
volaille
poultry
vol-au-vent
large puff-pastry case, also small individual-sized ones, filled with chopped poultry, fish or shell fish or vegetables in a *velouté* or *béchamel* sauce

Walewska, à la
crayfish and truffle garnish, with *sauce mornay*, for fillets of sole

Xavier
beef consommé flavoured with madeira, garnished with strips of pancake
xeres
sherry

yaourt
  yoghurt

zingara
  ('gypsy'), garnish, for veal and fowl, of white wine,
  mushrooms, tomato sauce and ham
Zola
  beef consommé, served with tiny cheese and truffle
  dumplings

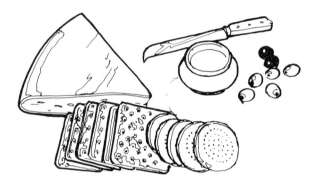

French Wines

The wines of France are infinite and varied. For the traveller this means constantly changing styles of wines, from the delicate and eminently quaffable wines of the Loire to the heavier, more robust and demanding wines of the Côtes du Rhone. What follows is a brief description of the most important wine growing areas, followed by a list of lesser known but nevertheless deserving areas. Wherever you travel in France you will come across growers and *négociants* offering the wines for tasting (*dégustation*) – this can be one of the best ways to get to know and appreciate the variety of wines that France has to offer.

Alsace & Lorraine

The much neglected wines of Alsace are now coming into their own. Choose carefully from an established shipper. The white wines are offered in styles based upon the grape from which they are made, the most notable being Gewurztraminer, Muscat, Riesling, Sylvaner, Tokay d'Alsace. The basic wine of the area is the Vin d'Alsace.

Champagne

Based around the two Champagne towns of Epernay and Reims, you will discover the most prestigious sparkling wine in the world. Many of the Champagne houses provide guided tours to view the Champagne process – not to be missed.

Loire

Delicious wines along a beautiful river. The whites of Saumur, Muscadet, Vouvray, Pouilly Fumé and Sancerre. As well as the light and refreshing reds of Chinon and Bourgeuil you will also enjoy the newly fashionable red Sancerre.

Burgundy

The gastronomic heart of provincial France. Red wines of the highest quality (and price) as well as probably the finest dry white wines in the world. There has been much upheaval in the Burgundy world in recent years, and quality is now variable – it was ever so. Careful buying is especially important and a respected and reputable *négociant* is vital.

Beaujolais

The great summer red wine – deliciously light and quaffable, perfect at any time, with almost any food. Some of the single village wines in good years will repay keeping.

Bordeaux

Along with Burgundy, the most famous red wine in the world. Produced from a classic mix of Cabernet Sauvignon, Merlot and Cabernet Franc grapes, the wines of this region have everything to offer, from the humblest Bordeaux *appellation* to the most exalted First Growth. Also the voluptuous and well-priced dessert wines of the Sauternes.

The Rhone

The wines of the Rhone are varied and often of quite superb quality. In the north the wines of the Côte Rotie, Hermitage, St. Joseph and Cornas. In the south Chateauneuf du Pape, Gigondas and the dessert wines from Beaumes de Venise. The white wine of Condrieu in the north should also be mentioned.

Other areas to note:

Bergerac
Cahors
Côtes Roussillon and Languedoc
Provence
Minervois and Corbières
Jurançon